Pterodactyls and Pizza

A Trumpet Club
Book of Poetry

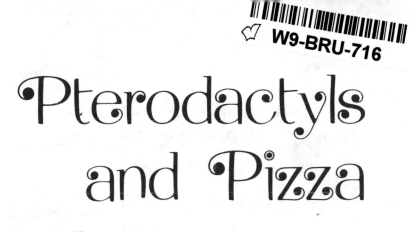

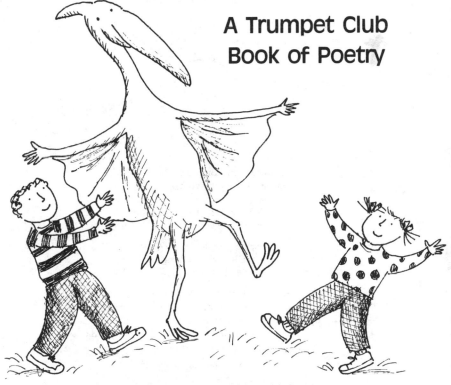

selected by Lee Bennett Hopkins
illustrated by Nadine Bernard Westcott

A Trumpet Club Original Book

to Bobbye S. and Gabe Goldstein—
Trumpeteers of Poetry

L.B.H.

to Becky and Wendy

N.B.W.

The acknowledgments on pages 93–96 constitute
an extension of this copyright page.

Published by The Trumpet Club
666 Fifth Avenue, New York, New York 10103

Collection copyright © 1992 by
Lee Bennett Hopkins
Illustrations copyright © 1992 by Nadine Bernard Westcott

ISBN: 0-440-84468-1

Printed in the United States of America
January 1992

10 9 8 7 6 5 4 3 2 1
CW

Contents

Introduction

Like music, poetry also sings, shouts, rings, and rages.

In this collection you will find a symphony of poems. Poems about people such as Lewis, who has a trumpet; a guy named Tony, who thinks boys are better than girls; and two girls who share a special friendship. Poems about living creatures who wiggle and laze, blink and wink, leap and sidle, spin and hide. Poems about the four seasons with their changing moments, from spring that sputters like bacon to frost that bites like a hungry shark. Poems about funny things to make you laugh, from a cereal box that is hard to open to a ravioli that you chew *sloli*. Poems about common, everyday things, from balloons that look like swollen creatures holding their breath to a clock that has lost its tick and tock. Poems about places: exploring a forest, living on a desert, singing about cities.

Have a good time reading this book.

Read it aloud, alone, or to a friend.

Try writing some poetry of your own.

Blast, blare, sing, shout your words on paper.

Happy Poetry-ing!

Lee Bennett Hopkins
Scarborough, New York

Sammy's Head Is Pounding

Poems About People

There are many people in our lives—
family members, people we know well,
and some we know but don't know well
at all.

Poets write about people—their feelings,
emotions, the way they act, and the things
they do.

Think about special people in your life.
How do they feel about a snowy or rainy
day? Do they like chocolate? Do they like
to sleep late or get up early in the
morning? Are they never on time?

Write a poem about someone you
know.

Lewis Has a Trumpet

A trumpet
A trumpet
Lewis has a trumpet
A bright one that's yellow
A loud proud horn.
He blows it in the evening
When the moon is newly rising
He blows it when it's raining
In the cold and misty morn
It honks and it whistles
It roars like a lion
It rumbles like a lion
With a wheezy huffing hum
His parents say it's awful
Oh really simply awful
But
Lewis says he loves it
It's such a handsome trumpet
And when he's through with trumpets
He's going to buy a drum.

Karla Kuskin

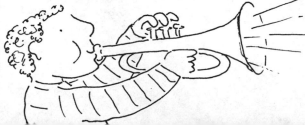

S.O.S.

Sammy's head is pounding—
Sammy's in pain—
A long division's got
Stuck in his brain—
Call for the locksmith
Call the engineer
Call for the plumber
To suck out his ear,
Call the brain surgeon
To pry out the mess,
Call out the Coast Guard
S.O.S.,
Because—
Sammy's head is pounding—
Sammy's in pain—
A long division's got
Stuck in his brain.

Beverly McLoughland

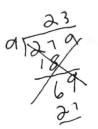

Girls Can, Too!

Tony said: "Boys are better!
  They can...

    whack a ball,
      ride a bike with one hand
      leap off a wall."

I just listened
  and when he was through,
I laughed and said:

    "Oh, yeah! Well girls can, too!"

Then I leaped off the wall,
  and rode away
With *his* 200 baseball cards
  I won that day.

Lee Bennett Hopkins

Two Friends

lydia and shirley have
two pierced ears and
two bare ones
five pigtails
two pairs of sneakers
two berets
two smiles
one necklace
one bracelet
lots of stripes and
one good friendship

Nikki Giovanni

Bobbin-Robin

James waved to Merilee
who waved to Kerrilee
who smiled at Sherilee
who cried to Sara Lee
do skate over to me.

Sara Lee ignored Sherilee
who shunned Kerrilee
who passed by Merilee
who knocked down James
skates and all.

James caught Merilee
who pulled down Kerrilee
who shoved Sherilee
who tripped Sara Lee
who cried like a baby.

Sherilee comforted Sara Lee
who pouted at Kerrilee
who chastised Merilee
who held on to James
with her little pinky.

So Mother took James
who held on to Kerrilee
who held hands with Merilee
who was talking with Sherilee
who was comforting Sara Lee
and they all skated home.

Patricia Corcoran Conway

13

Whispers

Kevin's whispers
buzz in my ear
like a buzzy old bee
too loud to hear.

Darcy's whispers
sound like a breeze
lost in the tops
of faraway trees.

Kathy's never
leave room for doubt
but *she* hasn't much
to whisper about.

Aileen Fisher

Flying Man

Flying-man, Flying-man
Up in the sky,
Where are you going to,
Flying so high?

Over the mountains
And over the sea,
Flying-man, Flying-man
Can't you take me?

Mother Goose

Some People

Isn't it strange some people make
    You feel so tired inside,
Your thoughts begin to shrivel up
    Like leaves all brown and dried!

But when you're with some other ones,
    It's stranger still to find
Your thoughts as thick as fireflies
    All shiny in your mind!

Rachel Field

In the Meadow
Green and Wide

Poems About
Living Creatures

Poets write about the wonders of living creatures—and why not? Each living thing is so different, unique in its own way, whether it is a new puppy waiting for you to come home from school, a spider magically spinning an intricate web, a bright-colored bird you've spotted in a park or in your own backyard, or a majestic horse standing alone in a field.

Choose a living creature to study. Then try writing about it.

New Puppy

I can't *wait*
for school to be over,
can't *wait*
to rush down the street,

For I
have a new brown puppy
with funny white socks
for feet.

He's the wiggliest
bundle of wiggles
you ever
could hope to see.

I can't *wait*...
and I hope my puppy
is waiting as hard
for me.

Aileen Fisher

Where Does
the Field Mouse Hide?

Where does the field mouse hide?
Here in the meadow green and wide.
What is she weaving
Deep in the grass?
A snug little nest,
A soft round mass.
The tight little house
With downy floor
Will nestle her babies
Seven or more.
The tiny mice will grow and hide
Here in the meadow green and wide.

Lillian M. Fisher

The Kittens

How limp they lie
all curled together,
as listless as
the August weather,
entwined in most
endearing poses
of arms and legs
and necks and noses...

It's hard to think
that on awaking
they'll be so fired
with mischief-making.

Aileen Fisher

Cat's Kit

Needle-like claws
Thimbled paws
Soft, silky, cushiony toes—

A
Siamese seamstress
wherever
           she
                   goes.

Lee Bennett Hopkins

Birds' Square Dance

Swing your partner
Cockatoo
Bluefoot booby
Marabou

Cassowary
Heel and toe
Toucan, noddy
Oriole

Chachalaca
To the right
Bobolink and
Hold her tight

Kittiwake and
Tap your feet
Loon and puffin
Parakeet

Flap your feathers
Curlew, crow
Pipit, tern, and
Do-si-do.

Beverly McLoughland

Five Little Owls

Five little owls in the old elm tree
Fluffy and puffy as owls could be,
Blinking and winking with big round eyes
At the big round moon that hung in the skies.

As I passed beneath, I could hear one say,
"There'll be mouse for supper, there will
      today."
Then all of them hooted, "Tu-whit, Tu-whoo!
Yes, mouse for supper,

      Hoo hoo. Hoo hoo!"

Anonymous

Sunning

Old Dog lay in the summer sun
Much too lazy to rise and run.
He flapped an ear
At a buzzing fly.
He winked a half opened
Sleepy eye.
He scratched himself
On an itching spot,
As he dozed on the porch
Where the sun was hot.
He whimpered a bit
From force of habit
While he lazily dreamed
Of chasing a rabbit.
But Old Dog happily lay in the sun
Much too lazy to rise and run.

James S. Tippett

One Little Colt

One little colt, alone on the hill,
heard the wind shout, "Run!"
So he ran down the hill.

One little colt, alone by the stream,
heard the water gurgle, "Go!"
So he dashed across the stream.

One little colt, alone by the wall,
heard the cow moo, "Leap!"
so he leaped across the wall.

One little colt, alone by the gate,
heard the goat blat, "Sidle!"
so he sidled through the gate.

One little colt, prancing through the heather,
heard one little boy shout,
"Now we're together!"

Patricia Hubbell

Spider

Spider's
spinning

Spider's
beginning

another web.

(Spin
low)

Thinning her long
and silky
thread

(Spin
high)

Spider's
spinning
her
silver lace.

Isn't her web
a lovely
place?

Ask fly.

Lilian Moore

Dinosaur

Final edition   In the index
under   D I N O S A U R
we find only
the out-of-print
bones

Once they were
a many-volume set   TRICERATOPS
and   BRONTOSAURUS   lived there
TYRANNOSAURUS REX   roamed
among the footnotes

In a back room
a few large books
remain   spines broken
and faded paper torn
A few legbones lie
scattered among the gluepots
beyond repair

D I N O S A U R   the ancient
lizard word   without
a publisher   copyright
expired

Barbara Juster Esbensen

Kindness to Animals

Riddle cum diddle cum dido,
My little dog's name is Fido;
    I bought him a wagon,
    And hitched up a dragon,
And off we both went for a ride, oh!

Riddle cum diddle cum doodle,
My little cat's name is Toodle;
    I curled up her hair,
    But she only said, "There!
You have made me look *just* like a poodle!"

Riddle cum diddle cum dinky,
My little pig's name is Winkie;
    I keep him quite clean
    With the washing machine,
And I rinse him all off in the sinkie.

Laura E. Richards

The Wind Sings

Poems About the Four Seasons

The four seasons—spring, summer, autumn, winter—are special times. Each one offers a host of new ideas to write about.

What is your favorite season of the year?

What makes it your favorite? Is it searching and finding new signs of spring? Swimming in a cool pool, ocean, or lake in the summer? Hopping through a pile of new-fallen leaves in autumn? Sledding or skiing in the middle of winter?

Write a poem about a special time you've had during a season—and share it with others.

Spring Is

Spring is when
    the morning sputters like
bacon
    and
       your
          sneakers
            run
               down
                  the
                     stairs
so fast you can hardly keep up with them,
and
spring is when
    your scrambled eggs
        jump
           off
             the
                plate
and turn into a million daffodils
trembling in the sunshine.

Spring

How pleasing—
not
to be
freezing.

Prince Redcloud

Springtime

in springtime the violets
grow in the sidewalk cracks
and the ants play furiously
at my gym-shoed toes
carrying off a half-eaten peanut
butter sandwich i had at lunch
and sometimes i crumble
my extra graham crackers
and on the rainy days i take off
my yellow space hat and splash
all the puddles on Pendry Street and not one
cold can catch me

Nikki Giovanni

A June Day in School

How can I add my numbers
when robins are flying by.

How can I spell my spelling words
when I hear the sea gulls cry.

My paper is turning wilder.
It won't do the same old things.

It jumps in my hands and I shape it
into a child with wings.

Sandra Liatsos

from
Stay, June, Stay!

Stay, June, stay! —
If only we could stop the moon
And June!

Christina G. Rossetti

Summer Night

Each night
my yard
is
the Fourth of July
lit up
by
sparkles
of

f   i   e   f   l   i   e
    r   s

Sue Thomas

Beaches

There are reaches of beaches
With nothing but sand
Where you go with a shovel
A pail and a friend
And you dig together
Well into the winter
The summer
The autumn
The former
The latter.
Years pass and you leave
Walking off hand in hand.
It doesn't much matter
How long you both dig there,
The sand will not end.

Karla Kuskin

Summer

What plans that we laid, and
What promises made, and
What dreams we created in May!
We vowed that we'd try to
Fill June and July, to
Have wonderful fun each warm day.
But while we were scheming,
Designing, and dreaming,
Our summer slipped quickly away!

Fran Haraway

End

Pack up
the
T-shirts,
sandals,
shorts.

Good-bye
to
the
ocean
and
my
sandcastle
fort.

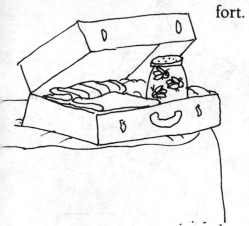

On
this
crisp,
brisk,
autumn-cool
day

it
is
time
to
pack
summer
neatly
away.

Lee Bennett Hopkins

Fall

When I go walking in the fall
I stop to watch the deer.
They open up their lovely eyes
And blink
And disappear.
The rabbits hop from here
To there
And in
And out
And under
While deep within the forest heart
The black bears roar like thunder.

The chipmunks gather butternuts
And hide them in a tree
Where clever squirrels
Discover them
And laugh with squirrelish glee.
My hat is green
My jacket blue
With patches on the sleeves
And as I walk
I crunch through piles
Of red and yellow leaves.

Karla Kuskin

Sleepy Schoolbus

Weekends, the battered yellow bus
  That calls at all our houses
And honks its horn to hurry us
  Draws shut its doors and drowses

Till, roused by Monday lunchbox smells,
  It yawns and reappears.
You look all worn out, yellow bus.
  Go home. Doze ten more years.

X. J. Kennedy

Halloween Moon

A chip of moon,
A broken bone
Is high and silent,
Cold, alone.
But ragged shadows
Dance a tune
The wind sings to
The white bone moon.

Fran Haraway

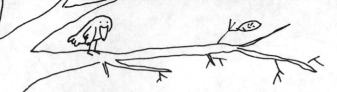

Wind Has Shaken Autumn Down

Wind has shaken autumn down,
left it sprawling on the ground,
shawling all in gold below,

waiting—

for
the
hush

of snow.

Tony Johnston

Christmas Time

I love the tinsel
I love the bells
I love the presents Santa Claus sells.

I love the red
I love the green
I love the Christmas trees I've seen.

But—

I hate the winter
I hate the sleet
I hate my cold and stinging feet.

I hate the wind and ice and grime.
Why can't Christmas come
In summertime?

Lee Bennett Hopkins

When Skies Are Low
and Days Are Dark

When skies are low
and days are dark,
and frost bites
like a hungry shark,
when mufflers muffle
ears and nose,
and puffy sparrows
huddle close—
how nice to know
that February
is something purely
temporary.

N. M. Bodecker

How to Talk to Your Snowman

Use words that are pleasing,
Like: freezing
And snow,
Iceberg and igloo
And blizzard and blow,
Try: Arctic, Antarctic,
Say: shiver and shake,
But whatever you *never* say,
Never say: *bake.*

Beverly McLoughland

March

A blue day,
a blue jay
and a good beginning.

One crow,
melting snow—
spring's winning!

Elizabeth Coatsworth

Where Are  My Pants?

Poems to Make You Laugh

Some poems can make you giggle. Some can make you laugh out loud.

Poets find lots of things to laugh about—from enjoying pasta to losing your pants!

Think of some funny things.

What if your teacher fell asleep during class?

What if your best friend got the hiccups during an important math test?

What if you lost your tooth in an apple at lunchtime?

Write a poem that will make you laugh—one that will make others laugh with you.

Have fun.

Laugh!

Ode to a Cereal Box

I strike,
I shred,
I smash,
I stab,

I rip,
I rend,
I grip,
I grab,

I jiggle,
jostle,
jolt,
and jab

But—

cannot
budge
the

"Lift this tab."

Fran Haraway

How to Assemble a Toy

This is the whatsit that fits on the knob
Of the gadget that turns the thingamabob.
This is the dingus that fits in place
With the doodad next to the whosiface.
This is the jigger that goes in the hole
Where the gizmo turns the rigamarole.
Now slip the ding-dang into the slot
Of the jugamalug, and what have you got?

It's a genuine neverwas such a not!

John Ciardi

Nightmare

Beautiful beautiful Beverly
Has asked me to a dance.
And I am dressed
In all my best:
My purple shirt,
My buckskin vest,
My cowboy boots,
My — oops!
Where are my pants?

Judith Viorst

The Spaghetti Nut

Eddie the spaghetti nut
courted pretty Nettie Cutt.
They wed and Ed and Nettie got
a cottage in Connecticut.

Eddie said to Nettie, "Hot
spaghetti I've just got to get."
So Nettie put it in a pot
and cooked spaghetti hot and wet.

Nettie cut spaghetti up
for Eddie in Connecticut.
Eddie slurped it from a cup,
that hot spaghetti Nettie cut.

Then Eddie, Nettie and their cat
that Nettie named Spaghettipet
all sat in the spaghetti vat—
so much for their spaghettiquette.

Jack Prelutsky

Italian Noodles

Whenever I
Eat ravioli
I fork it quick
But chew it sloli.

A meatballed mound
Of hot spaghetti
Is what I'm rarin' for
Alretti.

Why, when it comes
To pipelike ziti—
Well, I don't know
A sight more priti.

Wouldn't you love
To have lasagna
Any old time
The mood was on ya?

Oh why oh why
Do plates of pasta
Make my heart start
Fluttering fasta?

X. J. Kennedy

The Fabulous Wizard of Oz

The fabulous wizard of Oz
Retired from business becoz
    With up-to-date science,
    To most of his clients
He wasn't the wiz that he woz.

Anonymous

The Funny Old Man
and His Wife

Once upon a time, in a little wee house,
  Lived a funny old man and his wife;
And he said something funny to make
    her laugh,
  Every day of his life.

One day he said such a funny thing,
  That she shook and screamed with laughter;
But the poor old soul, she couldn't leave off
  For at least three whole days after.

So laughing with all her might and main,
  Three days and nights she sat;
And at the end she didn't know a bit
  What she'd been laughing at.

Anonymous

An Answer to the Question: How Old Are Fleas?

Adam
Had 'em.

Anonymous

A Monumental Bore

The nasty hornet doesn't mind
leaving monuments behind,
and if he lands upon you, kid,
he'll leave a little pyramid.

J. Patrick Lewis

Write About a Radish

Poems About Everyday Things

Balloons?
Bubbles?
A bottle of ketchup?
Do poets write about such things?
Of course they do.
Poets write about everything—from radishes to watering cans.

Try writing a poem about an everyday, taken-for-granted something.

How about paper clips, pterodactyls, pigtails, pepper, old pots—or even pizza pies?

Balloons

Twenty balloons in a cellophane sack—
Wrinkled and withered, misshapen and slack,
Limp, waiting rainbows at once promising
Marvels of happiness, laughter, and spring—
Bright hope for only a dollar a pack.

Fran Haraway

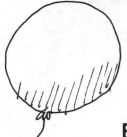

Balloons

Such swollen creatures,
Holding their breath
While they swim
Dreamily from
Room to room.

Swaying slightly,
They wander the air-wisps,
Bumping and rubbing along the walls
Until they feel their fat backs
Bob against the ceiling.

Wanting nothing,
They drift and sleep—
Bald as babies,
Smooth moons of blue and red,
Nodding drowsy, spellbound heads.

Deborah Chandra

Clock

This clock
Has stopped,
Some gear
Or spring
Gone wrong—
Too tight,
Or cracked,
Or choked
With dust;
A year
Has passed
Since last
It said
Ting ting
Or tick
Or tock.
Poor
Clock.

Valerie Worth

Ketchup

If you do not shake the bottle,
None'll come and then a lot'll.

Anonymous

from
Pencils

Pencils
telling where the wind comes from
open a story.

Pencils
telling where the wind goes
end a story.

Carl Sandburg

Sidewalks

A sidewalk is a wide walk
A let's-step-out-and-stride-walk
A two-abreast-let's-glide-walk
An arm-in-arm-let's-talk-walk
A pigeon-and-a-bug-walk
A shoulder-hugging-snug-walk
A hot-dog-and-balloon-walk
An under-sun-or-moon-walk
A grass-grows-in-the-crack-walk
A rainy-day-wet-track-walk
A place where you and I walk
And talk and talk and talk.

Patricia Hubbell

Until

Until
the new
hose
is
connected
there is
so
much
use
for
that treasured
old-weathered
watering can.

Lee Bennett Hopkins

Write About a Radish

Write about a radish
Too many people write about the moon.

The night is black
The stars are small and high
The clock unwinds its ever-ticking tune
Hills gleam dimly
Distant nighthawks cry.
A radish rises in the waiting sky.

Karla Kuskin

An Invitation

Poems About Places

Close your eyes.

Imagine a place you have visited or a place where you've never been.

Each place has its own personality—its own sight, smell, taste, touch, feel—the magic of a forest, the dryness of a desert, the rumble of a city.

Write a poem about a place—a place nearby or far away—a place that comes alive through poetry.

Sing a Song of Cities

Sing a song of cities.
If you do,
Cities will sing back to you.

They'll sing in subway roars and rumbles.
People's laughs, machines' loud grumbles.

Sing a song of cities.
If you do,
Cities will sing back to you.

Lee Bennett Hopkins

Forest: An Invitation

Mine the forest
left to travel,
Mine the bracken
to unravel.
Mine the creeping
wild grasses,
Mine the spongy
curling mosses,
Mine the hair
of shredding bark,
Ferns and fungus
nursed in dark,
Sunless paths
of rusty needles,
Algae film and
boring beetles,
Cups of lichen,
rotted stalk,

Flapping wings of
death's head hawk
Hushed by crowns
of skybound leaves
Hung from wild
woodland eaves,
Mine the foxglove
in the spring,
Mine the golden
toadstool ring,
Mine the tangling
claw and root,
Mine the snapping
twig and shoot.
Mine the bracken
to unravel,
Mine the forest
left to travel.

Myra Cohn Livingston

from

The Desert Is Theirs

This is no place
for anyone
who wants
soft hills
and meadows
and everything
green
green
green...

This is for hawks
that like only
the loneliest canyons
and lizards
that run
in the hottest sand
and
coyotes
that choose
the rockiest trails.

It's for them.

And for
birds
that nest
in cactus
and sing out over
a thousand thorns
because
they're where
they want to be.

It's for them.

And for
hard skinny plants
that do without water
for months at a time.

And it's for
strong brown Desert People
who call the earth
their mother.

Byrd Baylor

Oases

Oases
are places
in wide, sandy spaces
where date palms
grow dates
while the desert sun
blazes.
They sit there
in sunshine
so bright
that it hurts,
green date-plates
presenting
the desert's
desserts.

N. M. Bodecker

from
The Sea

The sea, the sea,
The rolling sea;
The endless waves
Are calling me.
The curling fingers
Beckoning,
Inviting as
The sea gull's wing.

The feeling swells
And I must go
To meet the tide
And feel the glow;
Remembering
The salt sea spray,
And sea gull's wing
Of yesterday.

Barbara M. Hales

Winter South

When cold, brisk winds begin to blow,
Please send me mountain-loads of snow.

    (I want more than gleam and glinter,
    More than a one-icicle-winter.)

Two feet sounds right, I suppose:
Enough to cause my school to close!

Isabel Joshlin Glaser

Back Home

It's snowing,
  and blowing,
And freezing the air.

It's hailing,
  and storming.

I'm glad I'm not there.

Let it come down.

Let it rip,
  let it roar.
'Cause I'm sitting
  with Grandpa
On the Florida shore.

Lee Bennett Hopkins

Index of Titles and Poets

Index of First Lines

Acknowledgments

Thanks are due to the following for work reprinted in this volume:

Patricia Corcoran Conway for "Bobbin Robin." Used by permission of the author, who controls all rights.

Curtis Brown, Ltd. for: "Back Home" by Lee Bennett Hopkins. Copyright © 1987 by Lee Bennett Hopkins. "Cat's Kit" by Lee Bennett Hopkins. Copyright © 1981 by Lee Bennett Hopkins. "Christmas Time" by Lee Bennett Hopkins. Copyright © 1972 by Lee Bennett Hopkins. "End" by Lee Bennett Hopkins. Copyright © 1992 by Lee Bennett Hopkins. "Girls Can, Too!" by Lee Bennett Hopkins. Copyright © 1972 by Lee Bennett Hopkins. "Sing a Song of Cities" by Lee Bennett Hopkins. Copyright © 1972 by Lee Bennett Hopkins. "Until" by Lee Bennett Hopkins. Copyright © 1985 by Lee Bennett Hopkins. All reprinted by permission of Curtis Brown, Ltd.

Farrar, Straus & Giroux, Inc. for: "Balloons" from *Balloons and Other Poems* by Deborah Chandra. Copyright © 1988, 1990 by Deborah Chandra. "Clock" from *Small Poems* by Valerie Worth. Copyright © 1972 by Valerie Worth. "Springtime" and "Two Friends" from *Spin a Soft Black Song* by Nikki Giovanni. Copyright © 1971, 1985 by Nikki Giovanni. All reprinted by permission of Farrar, Straus & Giroux, Inc.

Lillian M. Fisher for "Where Does the Field Mouse Hide?" Used by permission of the author, who controls all rights.

Isabel Joshlin Glaser for "Winter South." Used by permission of the author, who controls all rights.

Barbara M. Hales for an excerpt from "The Sea." Used by permission of the author, who controls all rights.

Fran Haraway for "Balloons," "Halloween Moon," "Ode to a Cereal Box," and "Summer." All used by permission of the author, who controls all rights.